PYRAMIDS

P E T E R   M E L L E T T

Gareth Stevens Publishing
A WORLD ALMANAC EDUCATION GROUP COMPANY

The original publishers would like to thank the following children,
and their parents, for modeling in this book: Steve Jason Aristizabal,
Ricky Edward Garrett, Sophie Halliström, Mitzi Johanna Hooper,
Imran Miah, Jessica Moxley, Kim Peterson, and Marlon Stewart.
Special thanks also to Bob Partridge for all his patient help.

Gareth Stevens Publishing would like to extend special thanks to Dr. Carter
Lupton for his expert assistance in verifying the accuracy of this text.
Dr. Lupton, an archaeologist and Head of the History Section at the Milwaukee
Public Museum, has participated in archaeological digs in the United States,
Europe, Syria, and Egypt and has led archaeological tours to Egypt, other
areas of the Middle East, and the Maya region of Central America.

Please visit our web site at: www.garethstevens.com
For a free color catalog describing Gareth Stevens' list
of high-quality books and multimedia programs,
call 1-800-542-2595 (USA) or 1-800-461-9120 (Canada).
Gareth Stevens Publishing's Fax: (414) 332-3567.

Library of Congress Cataloging-in-Publication Data

Mellett, Peter, 1946-
Pyramids / by Peter Mellett.
p. cm. — (Young scientist concepts and projects)
Includes bibliographical references and index.
Summary: Discusses the different kinds of pyramids, their structure,
construction, purposes, and creators. Includes related projects exploring
how pyramid shapes have many kinds of properties and uses.
ISBN 0-8368-2267-6 (lib. bdg.)
1. Structural engineering—Juvenile literature.   2. Pyramids—Design and
construction—Juvenile literature.   [1. Pyramids.]   I. Title.   II. Series.
TA634.M45   1999
909—dc21   98-34716

This North American edition first published in 1999 by
Gareth Stevens Publishing
A World Almanac Education Group Company
330 West Olive Street, Suite 100
Milwaukee, WI 53212 USA

Editor: Ann Kay
Consultants: Dr. Anne Millard and Jack Challoner
Photographer: John Freeman
Stylist: Melanie Williams
Designer: Caroline Grimshaw
Picture researcher: Annabel Ossel
Illustrators: Peter Bull Art Studio, Stuart Carter, Simon Gurr,
and Stephen Sweet/Simon Girling and Associates
Gareth Stevens series editor: Dorothy L. Gibbs
Editorial assistant: Diane Laska

Printed in the United States of America

3 4 5 6 7 8 9 05 04 03 02 01

PYRAMIDS

CONTENTS

WHAT ARE PYRAMIDS?

WHEN you hear the word "pyramid," what image comes into your mind? Perhaps you picture huge stone shapes and buildings that stand in Egypt by the great Nile River or in parts of Central America. Maybe you remember seeing some kind of pyramid shape at the top of a modern skyscraper. Perhaps you have looked through a microscope at tiny, pyramid-shaped crystals in a science class at school. There are many, many different kinds of pyramids all around us. Some pyramids are made by people; others are natural, but they all have one thing in common — the same special shape. All pyramids stand on a flat base and have flat, sloping sides, called faces. These sloping faces are always triangular in shape and meet at one point at the top of the pyramid. So, when you hear the word "pyramid," the first thing to think about is this special shape.

The most common kind of pyramid has a square, flat base and four sloping, triangular sides. Most pyramid-shaped buildings constructed during the last 5,000 years have this shape.

The Giza pyramids
These pyramids have been standing by the Nile River in northern Egypt for 4,500 years. They were built as tombs for great kings. The exteriors were once covered with a layer of smooth stone, but it was stolen by robbers.

The smooth limestone that once covered the exteriors of these pyramids is now missing.

Temple I, Tikal, Guatemala

This pyramid is in Central America, on the other side of the world from Egypt. It has steps up the outside and a temple at the top. Most Central American pyramids were built between 500 and 1,500 years ago.

Temple on top of pyramid

Canary Wharf, London

This tower was built during the 1980s. It has a pyramid at the top, which forms a striking landmark that can be seen for miles (kilometers). The pyramid shape is simple and dramatic, so it catches your attention. It has been used by many modern architects.

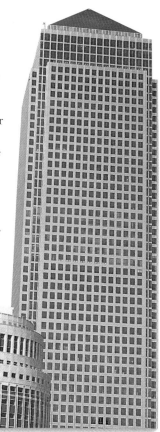

Spinel crystal

Not all pyramids are made by people. Pyramids can be found in the natural world, too. This crystal *(left)* is shaped like a pyramid. It is made of a mineral called spinel and was formed deep underground over many years. Natural crystals occur in a number of shapes. A salt crystal, for example, is shaped like a cube.

FACT BOX

• Egyptian pyramids were built from millions of stone blocks, or mud bricks encased in stone.

• Most Central American pyramids have a core of rubble, with stone blocks on the outside.

• Most Egyptian pyramids were built as tombs. Most Central American pyramids were used as temples.

PYRAMIDS AND MATH

THE kind of math that studies shapes is called geometry. Solid geometrical shapes include cubes, cones, spheres, cylinders — and pyramids. There is a whole family of different shapes we can call pyramids. The simplest member of this family is a pyramid with four faces, called a tetrahedron. It stands on a triangular base and has three other triangular faces. The next member of the family, called a square pyramid, has a total of five faces. It stands on a square base and has four triangular faces. You can make other pyramid shapes by adding more sides to the base and more triangular faces. You could make a pyramid with hundreds of faces, but most natural pyramids and pyramids built by people are either tetrahedrons or square pyramids. Every pyramid has two important measurements that describe its shape. The base length measures along one side of the base. The vertical height measures straight upward, from the middle of the base to the point at the top.

Cube

Sphere

Cone

Cylinder

Compare these different geometrical shapes (above) with a pyramid.

Solid model

Skeleton model

Square pyramid
A square pyramid stands on a square base. It is also called a regular pyramid because all the triangular faces are the same shape and size. A square pyramid has a total of eight edges.

Tetrahedron
A tetrahedron is a pyramid that stands on a triangular base and has three other triangular faces. It has a total of four faces and six edges.

Short and tall
Shapes like these *(left)* are also pyramids, although they might not look like pyramids at first glance. How many pyramid shapes do you see around you?

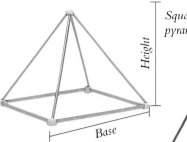

Square pyramid

Height

Base

Tetrahedron

Height

Base

The base length measures along one side of the base. The height measures from the point at the top straight down to the middle of the base.

Height of pyramids

Use straws and reusable adhesive to make a tetrahedron and a square pyramid. Measure them to learn about their shapes. It is easier to measure the height of a pyramid if you place the ruler in the center of the base.

The volume of a cube is base length x base length x height.

When you put a pyramid inside a cube, you will see that it takes up one third of the cube.

Volumes of pyramids

The volume of a shape is the amount of space inside it. Use straws and reusable adhesive to make a cube and a square pyramid with the same base length and height. The volume of the cube should be three times greater than the volume of the pyramid.

The volume of a square pyramid is ⅓ of base length x base length x height.

Tessellation

Some pyramid shapes tessellate, or fit together without any gaps. Experiment with small cardboard pyramids you make yourself or with the pyramid shapes from egg cartons.

SHAPE AND STRENGTH

You will need: modeling clay, ruler, plastic modeling knife.

WHY are pyramid shapes special? Why did ancient civilizations build gigantic pyramids rather than massive cubes or rectangles? The projects on these two pages will help you find out. The first project shows how a cube and a pyramid with the same base size and volume will differ dramatically in height. The second project shows that pyramids are much more rigid than cubes and do not collapse as easily. Seven hundred years ago, an earthquake destroyed the Egyptian city of Cairo, but nearby pyramids were hardly affected. So, if you want to build a sturdy structure with the smallest amount of material, build a pyramid. By the 1800s, construction materials had been developed for building tall, rectangular structures that are strong and stable.

Make a pyramid out of cardboard. Copy this shape onto a piece of cardboard. Cut it out, fold along the dotted lines, and glue the tabs together.

Bases and heights

3 Measure the cube and pyramid. They will have the same volume and the same size base, but the pyramid will be three times taller.

1 Make two cubes out of modeling clay. The faces must all be the same size, measuring 1½ to 2 inches (3.7 to 5 centimeters). Use a ruler to check your measurements.

2 Reshape one of the cubes to form a tall, square pyramid. Its base must be the same size as the original cube. You now have a cube and a pyramid.

A question of strength

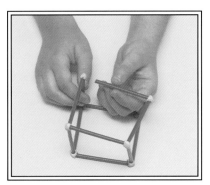

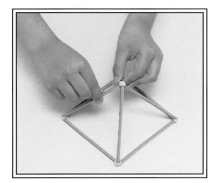

1 Use plastic drinking straws and reusable adhesive to make two models — a cube and a square pyramid. First, make the cube. Attach four straws to form the base.

2 Add eight more straws to complete the sides and top of the cube. Make sure the cube is even and that each face is the same size. Now, make a square pyramid.

3 The base should be the same size as the base of the cube. Attach four straws to make the base and add four more straws to form the faces of the pyramid.

MATERIALS

You will need: plastic drinking straws (cut in half), reusable adhesive.

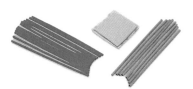

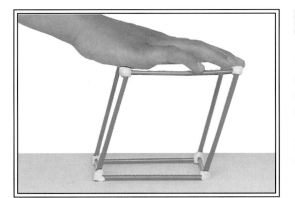

5 Do the same with the pyramid. Feel how much more rigid the pyramid shape is. It does not collapse because a pyramid has triangular-shaped faces that meet at a central point.

4 Push down gently with your hand over the center of the cube. Move your hand slightly to one side as you push and feel the cube start to collapse.

THE AGE OF PYRAMIDS

Fᴏʀ more than 4,500 years, people have been building huge pyramids all over the world. The oldest Egyptian pyramids were started more than 4,600 years ago. The newest pyramids in Central America were finished about 500 years ago. All these pyramids were connected in some way to the religions of the people who built them. Ancient Egyptians buried dead kings inside pyramids. The Aztecs, the Toltecs, and the Maya of Central America worshiped their gods in temples at the tops of pyramids. Huge, pyramid-shaped temples in Burma and Java are still used for worship today. Building these pyramids took a long time — sometimes over 50 years — and often involved thousands of people. Such a huge project is rare today.

Santa Cecilia, Mexico
The Santa Cecilia pyramid in Mexico has a flat top with a temple on it. This style is common in Central America.

Earth mound, North America
The Hopewell and Mississippian people of North America built temples or palaces on huge mounds of earth as big as 1,000 feet (300 meters) wide. Today, only grass-covered hillocks remain.

Temple of the Sun, Peru
This pyramid-shaped mound is called the Temple of the Sun. It was built by the Moche people in northern Peru nearly 2,000 years ago. It contains 143 million adobe bricks, which are bricks made from sun-dried mud.

		3000	2500	2000	1500
AFRICA		Aʀᴄʜᴀɪᴄ Pᴇʀɪᴏᴅ	[GIZA] Oʟᴅ Kɪɴɢᴅᴏᴍ — Eɢʏᴘᴛ	Mɪᴅᴅʟᴇ Kɪɴɢᴅᴏᴍ	Nᴇᴡ Kɪɴɢᴅᴏᴍ
NORTH & SOUTH AMERICA					Oʟᴍᴇᴄs
ASIA		Sᴜᴍᴇʀ		Bᴀʙʏʟᴏɴɪᴀɴs ᴀɴᴅ Assʏʀɪᴀɴs	Mɪᴅᴅʟᴇ Eᴀsᴛ

Hindu temple, Java

This Hindu temple at Prambanan, in Java, is over 1,000 years old. It has several pyramid-shaped roofs made from stone that has been carved into beautiful patterns. The Far East has many pyramid-shaped buildings.

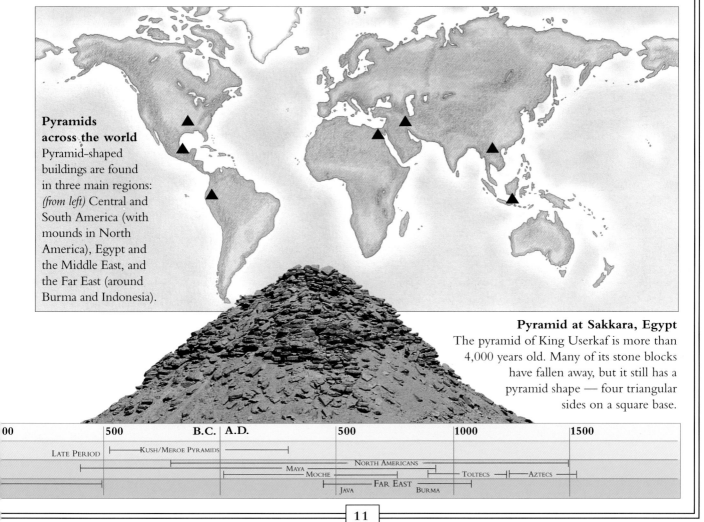

Pyramids across the world

Pyramid-shaped buildings are found in three main regions: *(from left)* Central and South America (with mounds in North America), Egypt and the Middle East, and the Far East (around Burma and Indonesia).

Pyramid at Sakkara, Egypt

The pyramid of King Userkaf is more than 4,000 years old. Many of its stone blocks have fallen away, but it still has a pyramid shape — four triangular sides on a square base.

00	500	B.C.	A.D.	500	1000	1500
LATE PERIOD	KUSH/MEROE PYRAMIDS					
			MAYA	NORTH AMERICANS	TOLTECS — AZTECS	
			MOCHE			
				FAR EAST		
			JAVA	BURMA		

11

UNCOVERING THE PAST

Modern archaeologists sift the earth looking for clues. They use tweezers and other delicate instruments, digging the ground with tiny trowels and moving sand away with soft brushes.

Archaeologists are people who try to understand the past by searching for ancient clues. They work very carefully, using special scientific instruments so they do not damage evidence. Today, they usually need permission from the government of the country they are working in before they can investigate a site. Permission, however, has not always been required, and, as recently as 100 years ago, archaeologists caused a lot of damage. They took away precious finds to fill museums and make themselves famous. They were no better than tomb robbers, who also have caused a great deal of damage. For thousands of years, robbers have assumed that, because the pyramids were built by rich, powerful rulers, there must be fabulous treasures hidden inside. They have broken into pyramids and taken away anything they wanted. Some have hacked into the stone looking for hidden tunnels. More recently, they have even used explosives. They have destroyed important clues about ancient life, which is why methods have to be so painstaking today.

Entering by force

This painting shows the terrible damage done by early archaeologists to Khafre's pyramid at Giza, in Egypt. King Khafre built his pyramid with a false door to mislead robbers. Archaeologists trying to find a way in used pickaxes and gunpowder to enlarge the entrance. This picture was painted in 1822, before photography came into widespread use.

The Grand Gallery

There is a steep passage inside Khufu's pyramid at Giza that leads to the burial chamber. This passage is called the Grand Gallery. It was sealed with huge stone blocks after Khufu's funeral, but, a few years later, tomb robbers broke through the blocks and stole everything.

This photograph was taken in 1910. It shows guides helping tourists climb to the top of Khufu's pyramid — 480 feet (146 m) above ground level. Today, authorities usually forbid this climb, because it is not safe, and it damages the stone.

Modern methods

Today's X-ray and scanning machines can look inside objects such as ancient Egyptian mummies. The ancient Egyptians preserved the bodies of their rulers by drying them and wrapping them in bandages. Modern machines, however, can see the skeleton beneath the wrappings.

Scanning machine

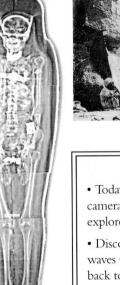

X ray

FACT BOX

• Today, tiny robots are used to take TV cameras into small spaces. For example, a robot explored shafts inside Khufu's pyramid.

• Discoveries can be made by beaming radio waves through soil and rock. The waves bounce back to the surface and reveal hidden chambers and passages.

13

The most impressive Egyptian pyramids that can be seen today are in the northern part of the region.

ANCIENT EGYPT

THE ancient Egyptian civilization began about 5,000 years ago and lasted 3,000 years. Its people lived on the fertile lands around the Nile River. Beyond this area, parched desert protected the country from warring neighbors. Compared to other places in the world, ancient Egypt was a very good place to live. Every year, the water level of the river rose and flooded its banks. The floodwaters brought huge amounts of fresh soil in which farmers grew plentiful harvests of food. The people believed that they were looked after by the gods especially well and that their king, called a pharaoh, was a god living on Earth. Egyptian priests said that when a king died, he must return to the sky and rejoin the gods. The king's pyramid was believed to be the place where his spirit left Earth and started its journey to the heavens.

Life along the Nile
This tomb painting *(left)* shows the Underworld, or the place where Egyptians believed people went after death. The Underworld was an idealized version of life in ancient Egypt, so paintings like this one give us an idea of what life was like on the shores of the Nile. You can see palm trees along the river and irrigation channels bringing water to the fields. At the top, on the left, a deceased person and his wife are worshiping various gods.

KING	DJOSER	SEKHEMKHET	HUNI		SNEFERU	KHUFU	KHAFRE	MENKAWRE	USERKAF
PYRAMID ▲ = PYRAMID	▲ STEP PYRAMID	▲ INCOMPLETE PYRAMID	▲ COLLAPSED PYRAMID		▲ BENT PYRAMID	⊢——— ▲ GIZA COMPLEX ———⊣			
DATES B.C.	2700 START OF THE AGE OF THE GREAT PYRAMIDS		2650		2600		2550		2500

◀——— 3000 B.C.: START OF ANCIENT EGYPTIAN CIVILIZATION.

Step pyramid of Djoser (Zoser) at Sakkara

The enormous step pyramid *(left)* built by King Djoser rises 195 feet (59 m) from the ground, in a series of six layers. It is the first pyramid and the oldest stone building in the world. At the beginning of ancient Egyptian civilization, mounds were built over graves. The more important the deceased, the larger the mound. Very large piles of stones and sand usually collapse and spread outward, but King Djoser solved this problem by using small stone blocks for his pyramid.

Collapsed pyramid of Huni at Meidum

This step pyramid *(left)* was built by King Huni. Notice how steep the sides are. Huni's son, Sneferu, added angled stones to the outside to make the first true, smooth-sided pyramid. Unfortunately, this casing crashed down, bringing much of Huni's pyramid with it.

Sneferu's bent pyramid at Dashur

When the pyramid built by Sneferu was half done, the builders realized that its sides were too steep. To keep the structure from collapsing, they made the top slope more gently.

SAHURE	NYUSERRE	UNAS		PYRAMIDS BECOME MUCH SMALLER IN SCALE. →
POOR QUALITY BUILDING— ONLY 4 OUT OF 14 PYRAMIDS SURVIVE		PYRAMID TEXTS		
2450	2400	2350	2300	100 B.C.: END OF ANCIENT EGYPTIAN CIVILIZATION. →

THE PYRAMIDS OF GIZA

GIZA, in northern Egypt, has some of the finest pyramids in the world. Among them are three kings' pyramids built by King Khufu, King Khafre, and King Menkawre. King Khufu's is the largest pyramid ever built in Egypt. Originally, it was 481 feet (146.6 m) high with a base approximately 758 feet (231 m) long. Khufu became king in 2589 B.C., near the start of the ancient Egyptian civilization, and he ruled for 23 years. Like all kings at that time, the first thing he did was decide where to build his pyramid tomb. Each king had to make sure his spirit could return to the sky when he died, and his pathway to heaven was his pyramid. The people believed that a deceased king continued to care for them from heaven. With that care, the Nile would continue to flood each year, and good harvests would grow. The building of Khufu's pyramid lasted throughout his reign and involved everyone in the kingdom in some way. Courtiers and priests from the palace controlled the work, while engineers, craftworkers, and thousands of peasants carried it out.

Pathway to heaven
Each of the three huge pyramids at Giza was linked to a chapel by a raised pathway, called a causeway. When a king died, his body was taken across the Nile by boat, transported along the causeway, and buried in his pyramid tomb. After the burial, a whole army of priests performed daily rituals to care for the king's soul. They thought the soul returned each day to the king's buried, preserved body.

Khufu

Khafre

Menkawre

The Sphinx

Granite quarry, Aswan

This granite quarry *(right)* is at Aswan, 600 miles (965 km) south of Giza. Pyramid builders mostly used soft limestone cut out of the ground at nearby quarries like this one. The chambers inside Khufu's pyramid, however, were lined with a polished stone called granite.

Transporting the stone

These boats on the Nile River are loaded down with large stone blocks. The stone used to build pyramids was carried down the Nile in very similar boats. Some of the granite blocks for Khufu's pyramid weighed over 50 tons (45 metric tons), as much as two large trucks.

The queens' pyramids

Each king at Giza had smaller pyramids built for his queens, next to his own. These three small pyramids *(below)* were built for Menkawre's three wives, although their tombs were never completely finished.

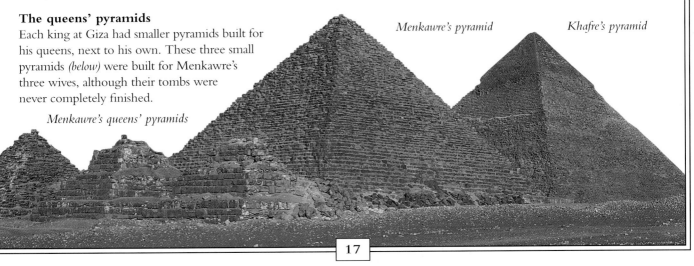

Menkawre's queens' pyramids

Menkawre's pyramid

Khafre's pyramid

PREPARING A SITE

M A T E R I A L S

You will need: string, modeling clay, wooden stick about 3 feet (1 m) long, tape measure.

MAKING precise measurements to construct a building is called surveying. Surprisingly, modern surveying equipment produces results no better than the equipment used by the Egyptians 4,000 years ago. The shape of Khufu's pyramid at Giza is amazingly accurate. Building an accurate pyramid requires just two things — the outside of the base must be level and the blocks must be laid absolutely flat, with their sides vertically straight. Pyramid builders used simple plumb lines to check that the verticals were straight, and they cut channels in the ground around the pyramid and filled them with water to check that the base was level. The projects on these two pages show simple ways to make and use a plumb line and a water level.

A modern plumb line. A plumb line is a weight on the end of a line. The weight holds the line straight.

Is it vertical?

1 To make a plumb line, tie a large knot in a piece of string and mold a ball of clay around it. The diameter of the ball of clay should be about 1 inch (2.5 cm).

2 Push a long stick into the ground, making it as vertical (pointing straight upward) as possible just by looking at it. Adjust the stick until you think it is straight.

3 To check how straight the stick is standing, ask a friend to hold your plumb line next to the stick while you measure between the stick and the line at both the top and further down. If the measurements are the same, the stick is vertical.

Is it level?

1 Make a simple version of a surveyor's level by nailing a short, flat piece of board to the top of a long wooden stick. Be careful with the hammer.

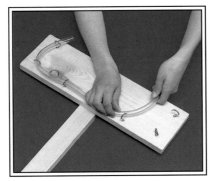

2 Screw in hooks across the bottom and up the sides of the short piece of board. Run plastic tubing through the hooks with about 1 inch (2.5 cm) sticking up over the top at each end.

3 Ask a friend to hold the level upright while you use a funnel to carefully pour water into the tubing. The water level in the tubing should be just above the piece of wood.

4 Have your friend hold a pole vertically about 16 feet (5 m) away. Look at the water lines of your level. When they line up with each other and with the pole, ask your friend to move a finger up and down the pole. Shout when the finger lines up with the water levels. Mark that point on the pole.

5 Repeat step 4 with the pole being held vertically at a different spot. The distance between the two marks on the pole shows the difference in level between the two places.

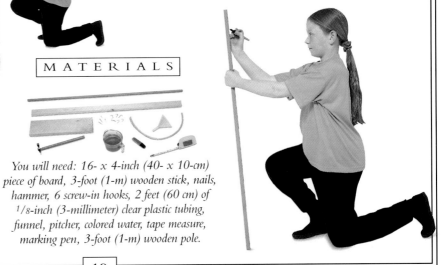

MATERIALS

You will need: 16- x 4-inch (40- x 10-cm) piece of board, 3-foot (1-m) wooden stick, nails, hammer, 6 screw-in hooks, 2 feet (60 cm) of 1/8-inch (3-millimeter) clear plastic tubing, funnel, pitcher, colored water, tape measure, marking pen, 3-foot (1-m) wooden pole.

BUILDING THE GREAT PYRAMID

I F you were helping to build the Great Pyramid (Khufu's pyramid) at Giza, you would take stone out of the ground by driving large wedges into cracks in the stone to split off smaller blocks. You would have to haul the blocks more than ½ mile (0.8 km) from the quarry to the building site. Each block would weigh over 2 tons (1.8 m tons). You would have to lift those blocks up more than 325 feet (100 m) to position them on the top layer of the growing pyramid. In ancient Egypt, wooden sledges and rollers were used to move the massive stone blocks more easily. Large wooden poles were used as levers to put the blocks in position. Up to 12 strong men were needed to move just one block on a sledge. At one point, 20,000 laborers were working on the Great Pyramid.

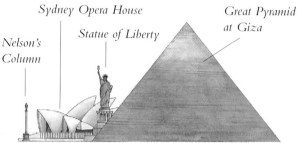

Nelson's Column *Sydney Opera House* *Statue of Liberty* *Great Pyramid at Giza*

The Great Pyramid at Giza is the largest stone building in the world. It is much larger than some of the world's most famous huge landmarks.

FACT BOX

• Khufu's pyramid was built from over two million blocks of stone. Each block is roughly the size of a kitchen table and weighs about 2.5 tons (2.3 m tons).

• The weight of Khufu's pyramid — about 5 million tons (4.5 million m tons) — is about the same as 250 large cruise ships.

The mysterious Sphinx
A huge, mysterious stone statue, called the Sphinx, guards the pyramids at Giza. It has the body of a lion and a human head and is a form of the Sun god. The Sphinx's head was carved from an outcrop of rock, and more rock was dug from the ground around that area to form the body.

King Khufu's chamber

Khufu's body was placed in this chamber, inside his pyramid. It is lined with red granite and stands at the top of a sloping shaft — the Grand Gallery.

The Great Pyramid is the only pyramid with passages inside as well as underneath. When workers finished this pyramid, they sealed off the Grand Gallery with stone blocks, then left through the escape shaft.

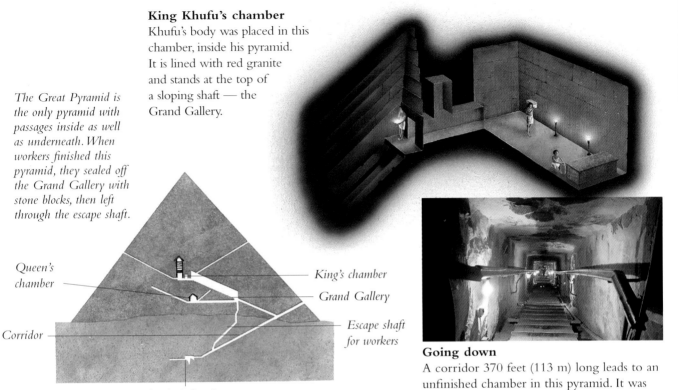

Queen's chamber

King's chamber

Grand Gallery

Corridor

Escape shaft for workers

Unfinished chamber

Going down

A corridor 370 feet (113 m) long leads to an unfinished chamber in this pyramid. It was bored in a straight line through solid rock.

Using ramps

This copy of a tomb painting shows that pyramid builders knew how to use a sloping ramp to make moving large loads, such as stone blocks, easier. They probably used a straight ramp almost 1½ miles (2.4 km) long leading to the top of the pyramid.

MOVING LOADS

M A T E R I A L S

You will need: a short ruler, a long ruler, 3 rectangular erasers (all the same size), a large potato (the load).

Levers are extremely simple devices that can be used to help lift all kinds of loads. Laborers working on the pyramids of ancient Egypt used levers made of wood to lift the enormous stone blocks into place. In the project on this page, you will find out how a lever can be used to turn a small amount of effort into a much larger force. In the projects on the opposite page, you will learn that cutting down on friction — a force that prevents things from sliding against each other — makes large loads easier to move. The ancient Egyptians used huge wooden rollers to cut down on friction when they moved their heavy loads. You can test this method yourself.

Conveyor belts with rollers are used in many modern warehouses. Like the ancient Egyptians, we still use simple ways of reducing friction, such as rollers, to make loads easier to move.

Using levers

1 Set up the materials *(as shown).* The eraser on the right is a pivot, or fulcrum; the long ruler is the lever. When you press on that end of the lever, you can easily lift the potato.

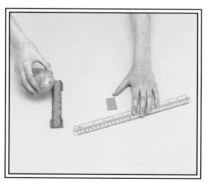

2 Move the fulcrum closer to the load. Even less effort is needed to lift the potato. The closer the fulcrum is to the load, the less effort is needed to lift it with the lever.

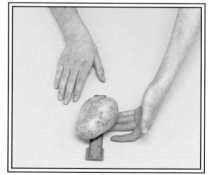

3 Try lifting the load using just your fingertips. Can you feel how much harder it is to lift without the lever? Experiment with different loads and levers and compare results.

Reducing friction

  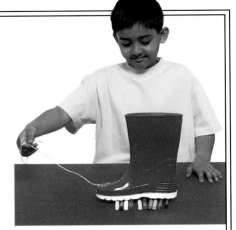

1 Tape a length of string to a boot and pull the boot, by the string, along a smooth surface. Pulling loads can be easier or harder depending on the surface.

2 Scatter sand on the surface and pull the boot over it. The boot moves more easily because the sand reduces friction. Each grain is like a tiny ball that rolls as the boot moves over it.

3 Place round pens or pencils in a row on the surface and pull the boot over them. Because these rollers are much larger than grains of sand, the boot moves even more easily.

Feeling the force

1 Tie string around the bundle of books (as shown). Attach a rubber band to the string and make two marks, about 1 inch (2.5 cm) apart, on it.

M A T E R I A L S

For "Reducing friction," you will need: a rubber boot, tape, string, sand, 9 round pens or pencils.

For "Feeling the force," you will need: heavy books wrapped up to form a bundle, string, strong rubber band, felt-tip pen, ruler.

2 Pull the bundle using the rubber band. You can find out how much the rubber band has stretched by measuring the distance between the two marks. This measurement gives you an idea of how much force was needed to pull the load.

PYRAMIDS AND MUMMIES

In the area around the Egyptian pyramids, there was a mortuary temple close to each pyramid. This temple was linked by a covered path to a valley temple near the river's edge.

ACCORDING to the religions of ancient Egypt, a king was a god who had come to live on Earth. All through his reign, the king prepared for the end of his life, when he would return to heaven. After death, his body had to be preserved as a mummy so it would not decay. First, the soft parts, such as the brain and internal organs, were removed. Next, the body was buried in natron, a kind of salt that dried out all the fluids that would cause it to decay. Then, the body was wrapped in bandages and was put into a wooden coffin. The king's *ka,* or spirit, was said to move between heaven and the pyramid tomb. The Egyptians believed that, as long as his body remained preserved, the king would continue to visit Earth. His people looked across the Nile to the pyramids and felt that their king was still watching over them from his tomb and that they were safe and secure.

A boat that looked much like the one in this picture (below) *was used to carry a king from his palace to the valley temple, where his body was dried out and wrapped so it would not decay.*

Receiving offerings

This statue of King Khafre *(left)* stood in the chapel linked to his pyramid. The Egyptians thought that, after death, a king's spirit reentered his body and any statues of him. So priests made offerings of food and drink, believing that the king could still enjoy them.

Canopic jar

The Egyptians used this type of jar *(left)* to store soft body parts, such as the stomach, which were removed from the body because they decay easily. This particular jar dates from some years after the age of the pyramids. It is shaped like a jackal.

Protected by the gods

This painting *(left)* shows a priest in a jackal mask attending to a mummy. The mask that the priest is wearing represents Anubis, the god of embalming, who protected the tombs and the mummies inside them. Turning the body of a great Egyptian king into a mummy was an elaborate procedure. At each stage of the process, priests and embalmers said special prayers and followed particular sacred rituals.

PRESERVATION

You will need: rubber gloves, 2 apples, 2 carrots, vegetable peeler, plastic garden tray with holes, newspaper, soil mix, stone, plastic object, piece of wood, spade.

Preserving something means stopping it from decaying. The Egyptians knew all about this and preserved their kings' bodies for many years. Decay results when invisible creatures, called bacteria, and tiny funguses, called mold, breed. Bacteria are everywhere. While we are alive, our bodies fight them. As soon as something dies, bacteria and mold start to cause decay. Bacteria grow best in moist places, so the Egyptians made a mummy by removing moist body parts and drying out the rest. Mummies were also wrapped in bandages soaked in oily resins that killed bacteria and molds — like modern antiseptics. Find out more by doing these projects.

King Seti I died over 3,000 years ago. This photograph of his mummy was taken in 1909. Archaeologists have cut off most of the linen bandages so you can see clearly how good the ancient Egyptians were at preserving bodies.

Learning about decay

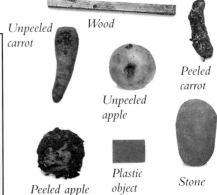

Unpeeled carrot

Wood

Unpeeled apple

Peeled carrot

Peeled apple

Plastic object

Stone

1 Peel one apple and one carrot. Line the garden tray with newspaper. Add a layer of soil mix and place the items *(pictured far right)* on it. Add more soil mix to cover the items.

2 Dig a shallow hole in a shady spot, put the tray in it, and cover it with earth so you can just see its top edges. Buried like this, the items will stay damp. Dig up the tray after a week.

3 Examine the items in the tray. Fruit and vegetables are attacked quickly by bacteria and mold, especially if they have no skin. Wood takes months to decay. Stone and plastic do not decay.

Preventing decay

1 Put one slice of bread into a plastic bag and seal the bag. Toast another slice of bread and seal the toast in another plastic bag.

2 Spread antiseptic ointment, which is designed to kill bacteria and molds, over one side of a third slice of bread.

3 Label each plastic bag. Set the bags in a warm place and check them once a day. What do bacteria and mold do inside the bags?

4 Bacteria and mold cannot grow on toast because there is no moisture. Antiseptic on the bread kills any germs. The plain slice of bread is very moldy.

Dry toast is not affected.

Chemicals in the antiseptic kill germs.

Plain bread gets very moldy.

MATERIALS

You will need: 3 slices of bread, 3 plastic bags with seals, antiseptic ointment, knife, 3 tags, pen, gloves.

5 Wear gloves when you handle the bags and do not open them when you look at the results. Keep the mold and bacteria wrapped safely inside the bags and drop them into a trash can.

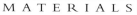

ANCIENT EVIDENCE

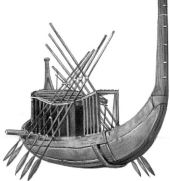

THE walls inside the pyramids at Giza are completely bare. There are no pictures, carvings, or writing. The first Egyptian king to have writing on the walls of the burial chamber inside his pyramid was Unas. King Unas lived about 250 years after Khufu (Khufu became king in 2589 B.C.). The writings that appear on the walls of Unas's burial chamber are known as the Pyramid Texts. These texts are not written in alphabet letters. Instead, the Egyptians used a kind of writing called hieroglyphs, in which each sound is represented by a picture. In later years, all Egyptian tombs were covered with these texts. Toward the end of the ancient Egyptian civilization, even the tombs of ordinary people had a small pyramid on top and texts on the walls. These texts tell us many interesting things about everyday life in the land of the great pyramids.

In 1954, Khufu's funeral boat (above) *was found in a pit* (below) *alongside his pyramid. The Egyptians thought his soul traveled across the sky in a boat.*

Unas's pyramid
The walls of this underground room in Unas's pyramid are completely covered with hieroglyphs that tell the dead king how to travel into the sky and meet the Sun god, Re.

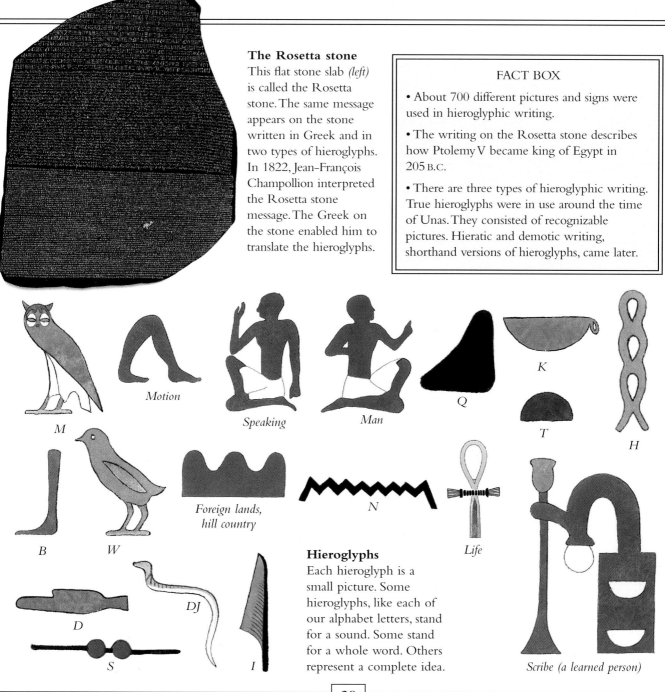

The Rosetta stone
This flat stone slab *(left)* is called the Rosetta stone. The same message appears on the stone written in Greek and in two types of hieroglyphs. In 1822, Jean-François Champollion interpreted the Rosetta stone message. The Greek on the stone enabled him to translate the hieroglyphs.

FACT BOX
• About 700 different pictures and signs were used in hieroglyphic writing.

• The writing on the Rosetta stone describes how Ptolemy V became king of Egypt in 205 B.C.

• There are three types of hieroglyphic writing. True hieroglyphs were in use around the time of Unas. They consisted of recognizable pictures. Hieratic and demotic writing, shorthand versions of hieroglyphs, came later.

M

Motion

Speaking

Man

Q

K

T

H

B

W

Foreign lands, hill country

N

Life

D

DJ

S

I

Hieroglyphs
Each hieroglyph is a small picture. Some hieroglyphs, like each of our alphabet letters, stand for a sound. Some stand for a whole word. Others represent a complete idea.

Scribe (a learned person)

USING SEALS AND PAINTS

You will need: modeling wax, warm water, potato, felt-tip pen, knife, envelope.

THE ancient Egyptians painted beautiful pictures and hieroglyphs on their walls, including the walls of some of their pyramids. They used powdered minerals for color and mixed them with a binder, such as egg white or gum, to make paints. They also placed seals on the doors of tombs and on chests, so people could not get into them easily. Egyptian seals were made of mud. Many years later, people around the world were using seals on private letters, but these seals were made of wax. The project on this page shows how to make an attractive seal for your own letters. You will learn how seals work and how to make a pattern in your seal. The project on the opposite page shows how to make paints similar to those used by the Egyptians. Perhaps you would like to paint your own scene of everyday life in ancient Egypt, or you might try painting some hieroglyphs.

Experiment with different designs for your personal seal.

Make your own seal

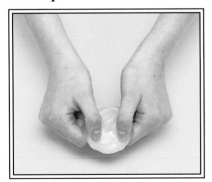

1 Drop modeling wax into warm water for a few minutes. Squeeze it with your fingers until it is very soft. Let it sit in warm water while you do the next step.

2 Cut a potato in half. Draw a design on one half and have an adult help you carve out the design with a knife. The design should stand out *(as shown in the close-up above).*

3 Take the wax out of the water and drop it onto the flap of the envelope. Press the potato into the wax. Then lift it off to reveal your seal.

Ancient painting methods

1 Paint color comes from powders called pigments. The Egyptians used powdered minerals. Use colored chalk and charcoal to make your pigments. Crush them on a plate with a spoon.

2 Mix the pigment with a binder, such as egg white. Then stir the egg white, water, and pigment together until you have a thick, strong paint.

3 To make a paintbrush, cut pieces of straw and put them together in a bundle about $1/4$ inch ($1/2$ cm) thick. Ancient Egyptians also used straw to make their paintbrushes.

MATERIALS

You will need: colored chalk, charcoal sticks, spoon, egg, 2 small dishes, water, straw, rubber band, pen, scissors, paper.

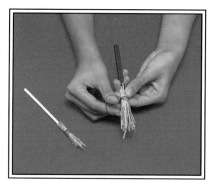

4 Use a rubber band to attach the bundle of straw to the end of a pen. Trim the brush with scissors to make the tip pointed. Make more brushes of different sizes.

5 Use your paints and brushes to create a picture. To be as much like an ancient Egyptian picture as possible, your painting should be in browns, yellows, black, and white.

Try painting pictures of Egyptian hieroglyphs.

PYRAMIDS AND THE STARS

This painting is from the ceiling of a king's tomb. It shows several important Egyptian gods and their stars in the night sky.

THE three enormous pyramids at Giza hold many secrets. Although they are empty, they are filled with hidden meanings. Most of these meanings are linked with stars in the sky. The Egyptians thought that each star was actually a different god. When a king died, his spirit returned to the sky and lived there in the form of a star. The three Giza pyramids are laid out on the ground in the same pattern as the stars known as Orion's belt. Also, the four passages in Khufu's pyramid pointed exactly at the four stars that represented the four most important Egyptian gods. It seems that the ancient Egyptians knew a great deal about the stars.

Finding north and south by the stars

Before a pyramid was built, a priest set the north-south line, using a curved wall and a forked stick. He noted where a star rose above the wall and where it set, farther along the wall. The north-south line ran from the forked stick to a point halfway between where the star rose and set. The base of Khufu's pyramid is laid out facing exactly north-south and east-west. It is so exact you would think it had been laid out with modern instruments.

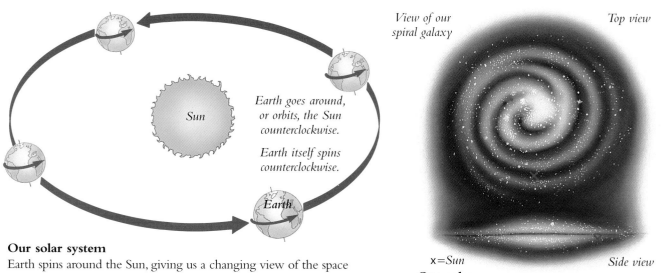

View of our spiral galaxy *Top view*

x=*Sun* *Side view*

Our solar system

Earth spins around the Sun, giving us a changing view of the space around us. Earth itself also spins around once a day, so the Sun seems to move across the sky. At night, the stars appear to move in curved paths. Some of the brightest points of light are the planets Mars, Venus, and Jupiter, lit by the Sun. Ancient Egyptians might have used these planets to find the north-south line.

Earth goes around, or orbits, the Sun counterclockwise.

Earth itself spins counterclockwise.

Our galaxy

Our Sun is actually a star. It is one of billions of other stars arranged in a spiral, called a galaxy. The Sun is near the rim of this galaxy. There are billions of other galaxies in the universe, far away from ours. We cannot see the stars during the day because the Sun is so bright.

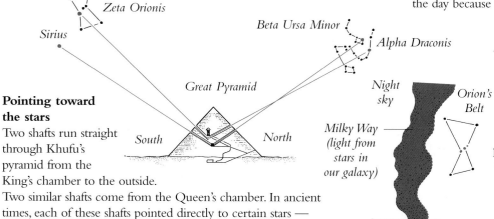

Zeta Orionis

Sirius

Beta Ursa Minor

Alpha Draconis

Great Pyramid

South *North*

Night sky

Orion's Belt

Milky Way (light from stars in our galaxy)

Nile River

Pointing toward the stars

Two shafts run straight through Khufu's pyramid from the King's chamber to the outside.
Two similar shafts come from the Queen's chamber. In ancient times, each of these shafts pointed directly to certain stars — the homes of important gods and goddesses. The pattern of stars in the sky has changed since the pyramid was built, but computers can show how the stars appeared in Khufu's time.

The pyramids and the stars

Some people have suggested that, at Giza, the Nile River forms a shape similar to the Milky Way in the night sky overhead. Also, the three Giza pyramids are arranged a lot like the three stars in the middle of a group of stars called Orion's Belt. The Egyptians may have been trying to make a place on Earth for their gods, who lived in the stars.

33

FINDING NORTH AND SOUTH

You will need:
globe, toothpick, modeling clay,
lamp, masking tape, scissors,
tape measure.

KHUFU'S pyramid at Giza was constructed in an amazingly accurate way. Its massive base is almost a perfect square, and the sides of the base point exactly north-south and east-west. The ancient Egyptians did not have magnetic compasses to find north and south as we do today. Instead, they used the stars. The projects on these two pages show you how to use the Sun, which is just a very large star, exactly the same way. First, you will use a model to help you understand some basic principles. Then, you can try the real thing outdoors. In the first project, the first shadow you mark represents the shadows you see in the middle of the morning. The second shadow you mark represents the shadows that fall mid-afternoon. The lamp represents the Sun, which casts the shadows. Turning the globe represents how Earth rotates each day.

Finding north

1 Stick a toothpick vertically into clay over Egypt. Point a lighted lamp (the Sun) at the globe. Turn the globe until a shadow appears. Mark it with tape.

2 Turn the globe until you see another shadow, the same length, pointing in the opposite direction as the first one. Mark this shadow, also.

3 Now, join the ends of these two pieces of tape with another piece of tape. Measure the third piece of tape to find its center. Mark this point.

4 With more tape, mark a line from Egypt (at the base of the toothpick) to the center of the third piece of tape. This line points exactly to the North Pole.

Moving outside

1 On a bright, sunny day around mid-morning, push a stick vertically into the ground. Use a plumb line to check that the stick is vertical.

2 The stick will cast a shadow on the ground. Cut two paper strips exactly the same length as the shadow. Place one paper strip on the ground directly under the shadow.

3 As time goes by, the shadow will move and change length. Later in the afternoon, it will be the same length as the second paper strip. Mark this shadow with that strip.

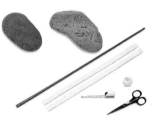

4 Just as you did with the globe model in the first project, join the two ends of the paper strips. An effective way to do it is with string wrapped around and held down with stones.

5 Measure to find the middle of the string. Join this point with the bottom of the stick. The line will point exactly north-south, just like it did on the globe model.

CENTRAL AMERICA

Besides Egypt, another main region of the world where pyramids are found is Central America, which is the land from Mexico down to the northern part of South America. Ancient Egypt was cut off from its neighbors by deserts and the sea, and one distinct group of people lived there. In Central America, however, there were many different groups of people, such as the Olmecs, the Toltecs, the Maya, and the Aztecs. Over thousands of years, these groups moved back and forth, fighting and conquering each other. The pyramids in this region are less than half as old as the ones in Egypt. Most were built between 1,500 and 500 years ago. Unlike most Egyptian pyramids, the pyramids in the Americas have wide staircases running up the outside to a temple at the top. In Egypt, the pyramids have stood undisturbed in the desert for thousands of years. In Central America, explorers have often found pyramids half buried, deep inside hot, steaming jungles.

Most American pyramids are in Central America, which is the area that links North America with South America.

Sun pyramid, Teotihuacan
The Pyramid of the Sun *(left)* was built around A.D. 300 at Teotihuacan, near what is now Mexico City. It has a solid core made with millions of sun-dried mud bricks. The outside is covered with blocks of hard stone.

		LAST EGYPTIAN PYRAMIDS	500	B.C. ◄——— 0 ———► A.D.
MEXICO				
YUCATÁN PENINSULA				
NORTH AMERICA				HOPEWELL │ PEOPLE

Pyramid of the Magician, Uxmal, Mexico

This pyramid *(right)* on Mexico's Yucatán Peninsula was built in at least five stages sometime between A.D. 500 and A.D. 900. An impressive main stairway leads to the top and to one of the pyramid's five superimposed temples. This pyramid is unusual because it has curved walls. Uxmal was once a prosperous town filled with grand buildings. It flourished between about A.D. 600 and A.D. 1000.

Temple of the Inscriptions, Palenque

This temple pyramid *(above)* was built by the Maya in southern Mexico about 1,200 years ago. It is one of very few pyramids in the Central American region that was used as a tomb. The sarcophagus, or coffin, found buried inside had a beautifully carved lid *(pictured on page 41)*.

Tula, Mexico

This pyramid at Tula *(below)*, like most Central American pyramids, does not rise to a point. A temple once stood at the top. Tula was the capital of the Toltec empire.

500	1000	1500
CITY OF TEOTIHUACAN	TOLTECS	AZTECS
MAYA		

WORKING WITH ROCK

*You will need:
round-ended knife, block of oasis
foam (used by flower arrangers),
foam concrete (fairly soft)
building block.*

THE major pyramids were made from rock, or stone, because it lasts much longer than earth or bricks. Building them meant cutting huge amounts of rock out of the ground and carving it. There are three main types of rocks: sedimentary, igneous, and metamorphic. Sedimentary rocks formed long ago, when particles of sand or tiny animal shells built up in layers under the sea. Igneous rocks formed near volcanoes, when molten rock cooled and became solid. If igneous and sedimentary rocks are later heated underground, they change into metamorphic rocks. Some rocks are hard; others are much softer. Certain rocks have beautiful patterns and colors in them. The Central Americans used a lot of granite, an igneous rock, in their buildings. The ancient Egyptians used lots of limestone, a sedimentary rock. In both cultures, rock was carved with simple hammers and chisels. The projects on these two pages will help you take a closer look at rocks and discover some of their properties.

Cutting and carving

1 Could you be a sculptor? Practice etching a simple shape on a block of oasis foam. Have an adult help you cut around it with a blunt knife. Is this material easy to cut?

2 Repeat step one with the foam concrete building block. This block is much harder than oasis foam, but it is softer than actual stone.

Now that you know how hard it is to carve material that is much softer than stone, how long do you think it would take you to carve real stone with only simple tools?

Learning about rock

1 Do a vinegar test to help find out what kinds of rocks your samples are. Put a few drops of vinegar on each rock sample and watch what happens.

2 Limestone, chalk, and marble make vinegar fizz. It reacts this way because these rocks are types of calcium carbonate. Common rocks, such as flint, granite, and sandstone, are not affected by vinegar.

3 Scratch one rock sample with another. Harder rocks leave marks on softer rocks. Hardness also helps identify rocks. Think how difficult it must be to carve the harder rocks.

Flint

Granite

Limestone

Sandstone

MATERIALS

You will need: vinegar, spoon, rock samples, magnifying glass, geology reference book.

You can see small crystals in granite.

5 Use a magnifying glass to compare your rocks with pictures in a geology reference book. Igneous rocks have sharp crystals in them. Metamorphic rocks look smooth. Sedimentary rocks have layers and tiny bits in them.

4 Arrange your rock samples in order of hardness. Igneous rocks, such as granite, are usually the hardest. Sedimentary rocks, such as sandstone, are usually the softest.

THE MAYA PEOPLE

THE Maya have lived in the Yucatán peninsula area of Central America for more than two thousand years. At the height of their civilization, between about A.D. 250 and A.D. 1000, they built spectacular pyramids. Maya pyramids were aligned north-south very accurately, and, from the tops of their pyramids, the Maya made careful measurements of how the sun, moon, and stars moved. The Maya were fascinated by time and drew amazingly complicated calendars, based on their observations of the stars. Our calendar covers 365 days and has an extra day every leap year. One of their calendars covered 52 years and followed the stars more accurately than ours. Every day was linked to a different god. Each god required its own special prayers and offerings. Various circumstances brought about the end of the Maya civilization. One of the main reasons was probably fighting between the rulers of the different city-states.

This carved head shows how Maya people looked long ago. Many of the Maya people living in Central America today have very similar features.

FACT BOX

• The Maya used several different calendars. A 260-day calendar is still used in some remote regions of Central America today.

• Inside the famous El Castillo pyramid at Chichén Itzá is another, smaller pyramid. This inner pyramid was constructed about a hundred years before the one we see today. *El Castillo* means "castle" in Spanish.

Grand Plaza, Copán, Honduras
This pyramid *(left)* is at Copán, one of the main locations used by Maya astronomers. Like the Egyptians, the Maya believed that life on Earth is controlled by the way the stars move. They believed that their calendars could predict the future.

Palenque, southern Mexico

The Temple of the Inscriptions stands on the top of this pyramid *(right)*. Its walls are covered with strange writing and carvings. In 1949, workmen removed a stone slab from the floor and found a stairway that leads down inside the pyramid to a burial chamber. The remains of six people who had been sacrificed and a great carved stone coffin with a beautiful lid *(below right)* were found inside the chamber.

Tomb lid from the Temple of the Inscriptions

The lid of the coffin buried under the Temple of the Inscriptions weighs 5 tons (4.5 m tons). Its carvings show a Maya lord surrounded by sacred symbols, such as a dragon. These carvings have taught us many things about how the Maya lived.

El Castillo, Chichén Itzá, Yucatán Peninsula

This magnificent pyramid *(above),* built around A.D. 1100, is the largest in the Maya city of Chichén Itzá. The number of steps up the sides and in the temple equals 365 — the number of days in a year.

THE CITY OF TEOTIHUACAN

TEOTIHUACAN is an enormous ancient city that lies 25 miles (40 km) northeast of Mexico City. At the end of the 1800s, it was a crumbling mass of overgrown ruins and half-buried pyramids. Today, however, it is one of the world's greatest ancient sites. Hundreds of thousands of tourists visit every year. Around A.D. 500, Teotihuacan, with a population of about 120,000, was one of the largest cities in the world. About one third of the population were skilled craftspeople, and there were more than eight hundred workshops supplying tools, knives, statues, and pots to the city and surrounding countryside. All the city streets were laid out on a square grid, just like modern New York City. Running through the center of the city was a wide road called the Street of the Dead, which is still there today.

The Street of the Dead
At one end of this road *(above)* is the pyramid Temple of Quetzalcoatl. At the other end is the Pyramid of the Moon. Halfway between them is the huge Pyramid of the Sun.

Staircase, Temple of Quetzalcoatl
This staircase *(above)* runs up the side of the Temple of Quetzalcoatl. It is lined with carvings of jaguar heads. Jaguars represented the fertility of the earth. Rulers wore jaguar skins as symbols of power.

FACT BOX

• An engineer who studied Teotihuacan very closely during the 1960s concluded that the Street of the Dead was actually a scale model of the solar system.

▲ The Temple of Quetzalcoatl is the Sun.

▲ Markers along the street represent the inner planets Mercury, Venus, Earth, Mars, and Jupiter.

▲ The Pyramid of the Sun represents the planet Saturn.

▲ The Pyramid of the Moon is Uranus. (Note that Uranus was unknown to Western astronomers until 1781.)

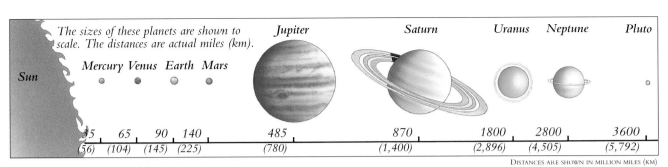

The sizes of these planets are shown to scale. The distances are actual miles (km).

Sun	Mercury	Venus	Earth	Mars	Jupiter	Saturn	Uranus	Neptune	Pluto
	35	65	90	140	485	870	1800	2800	3600
	(56)	(104)	(145)	(225)	(780)	(1,400)	(2,896)	(4,505)	(5,792)

DISTANCES ARE SHOWN IN MILLION MILES (KM)

Our solar system consists of the Sun and the planets. Some archaeologists have thought that the Street of the Dead, in the ancient city of Teotihuacan in Mexico, mirrors the solar system.

Pyramid of the Moon

From the top of this pyramid *(right)*, the view of Teotihuacan and the Street of the Dead is magnificent. Like all buildings in this city, the pyramid was once painted with patterns and scenes. Imagine how bright and colorful the city must have been at that time.

Pyramid of the Sun

The base of the Pyramid of the Sun is 700 feet (213 m) long. The pyramid is 230 feet (70 m) high and has a volume of 35 million cubic feet (1 million cubic meters). The mud used to make the sun-dried bricks would have filled 5,000 Olympic-sized swimming pools. The pyramid was built in four huge steps. At the corner of each step, excavators found the skeleton of a person who had been buried alive.

THE TOLTECS

THE Toltecs were a warring race. The great days of their civilization followed after most of the Maya cities had started to decline. They attacked and looted Teotihuacan and the surrounding lands in about A.D. 750, and Toltec influence also seems evident in the Maya city of Chichén Itzá. Chichén Itzá is famous for the huge pyramid El Castillo. As time went by, the Toltecs repaired old pyramids and temples and built many new ones. They used stones or bricks made from sun-dried mud for the insides and covered the outsides with slabs of smooth stone. Like all Central American pyramids, there were staircases up the sides and temples at the top. As the Toltecs conquered more places, they became more ferocious. They believed that their gods needed blood and thought that human sacrifice was the only way to keep the Sun burning. The sacrifices were made in the temples at the tops of the pyramids.

In Chichén Itzá, 1,000 years ago, the main building was the pyramid El Castillo, which towered over the main square. The Toltecs had great influence over the area around Chichén Itzá and might have ruled there.

Chacmool figure

A stone figure, called a Chacmool *(left)*, was found at the top of El Castillo. Similar figures were found at various sites in the Americas. Each Chacmool has a plate on its belly. The Toltecs believed that their god Quetzalcoatl had sacrificed his heart and blood to make the Sun. To keep the Sun burning, Toltec priests cut out the hearts of human victims and piled them onto Chacmool's plate.

44

Temple of the Warriors, Chichén Itzá

This temple *(left)* is surrounded by sixty carved columns. The carvings show the weapons used by Toltec warriors. The warriors were split into groups — the Eagles, Jaguars, and Coyotes — and wore huge, feathered headdresses.

Caracol observatory, Chichén Itzá

The Caracol observatory *(right),* a building for looking at the night skies, was built by the Maya but was also used by the Toltecs. Its windows and pillars line up with the planet Venus. To the Maya and the Toltecs, Venus was closely linked to the Sun, which was also extremely important to their beliefs.

Cenote of Sacrifice, Chichén Itzá

This massive well *(left)* measures 200 feet (61 m) across. Steep, rocky sides drop down to murky water 65 feet (20 m) below. All kinds of offerings — even people — were thrown into this well. In 1962, divers brought up over 4,000 objects, including gold disks that showed various scenes from Maya and Toltec religious rituals.

HOW BIG?

You will need: 4 large stones, 4 balloons, string, scissors, compass, tape measure.

MOST of the world's pyramids are huge. The largest — the Great Pyramid at Giza — is 481 feet (146.6 m) high and has a base length of approximately 758 feet (231 m), which means that each side of the Great Pyramid is about 2½ times longer than a 100-yard (91.5-m) race track. The Great Pyramid covers an area of 13 acres (5 hectares) — the same as nearly seven soccer fields. The projects on these two pages use the El Castillo pyramid at Chichén Itzá to help you understand the gigantic size of a pyramid. The first project shows how to measure out the actual size of the pyramid's base. In the second project, you can make a scale model of El Castillo.

To use your feet for measuring distances in the first project, find out how many foot-lengths equal one yard (m).

A life-size pyramid

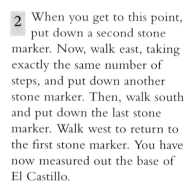

1 In an open space, put down a stone marker (a large stone with an inflated balloon tied onto it). Using a compass, walk north, taking the number of heel-to-toe steps that equals 55 yards (50 m).

2 When you get to this point, put down a second stone marker. Now, walk east, taking exactly the same number of steps, and put down another stone marker. Then, walk south and put down the last stone marker. Walk west to return to the first stone marker. You have now measured out the base of El Castillo.

El Castillo, Chichén Itzá

The project on the opposite page gave you an idea of how big El Castillo is. This picture *(right)* shows how big it is compared to people. It is still, however, much smaller than the Great Pyramid at Giza! In the following project, make a scale model of El Castillo and compare it with a model car.

Scale model of El Castillo

1 This model car is 2 inches (5 cm) long. A real car might be 11½ feet (3.5 m) long. We say that the scale of the model car is 1:70 (1 to 70). In other words, the real car is 70 times longer.

3 Hold up the strings that form the sides of the pyramid and place the model car next to it to see how large a real car would look next to El Castillo. You can make a model of Khufu's pyramid, too. If you make it to the same scale, its base sides would be 10 feet (3 m) long and its height would be 7 feet (2 m).

2 Use stones and string or cord to make a 1:70 scale model of El Castillo *(as shown)*. The base should be 31 inches (77.5 cm) long (2200 ÷ 70). The sloping sides should measure 16 inches (40 cm) long.

THE AZTECS

THE Aztecs came after the Toltecs. They were the last major civilization in Central America and the last people to build pyramids in that region. Their nation was at its peak between about A.D. 1400 and A.D. 1519. Their capital city was Tenochtitlan. In 1519, soldiers from Spain invaded, and swiftly defeated, the Aztecs; thus, Spanish became the main language of Central America. Like the Maya, the Aztecs had calendars based on the movement of the stars. Priests studied the calendars and predicted eclipses of the sun and moon, as well as the end of the world. Like the Toltecs, the Aztecs believed that the only way to stop the end of the world was to sacrifice humans. Many of these sacrifices took place in the pyramid temples. Disapproving of the sacrifices, the Spaniards tried to convert the Aztecs to Christianity.

Tenochtitlan was built on an island in Lake Texcoco. This map (above) was drawn by Spanish invaders. It shows the El Templo Mayor pyramid in the center of the city.

FACT BOX

• The El Templo Mayor pyramid in Tenochtitlan was built in seven layers over two centuries. Each new layer encased the older versions of the temple.

• Aztec myths said that the god Quetzalcoatl would return from the west as a pale-skinned, bearded man. Cortés, the Spanish conqueror, fit this description, so his conquest of the Aztecs was fairly easy.

Cortés and Moctezuma, in 1519
This Spanish painting *(right)* shows the Aztec leader Moctezuma welcoming the Spanish leader Hernándo Cortés to Tenochtitlan in 1519. Moctezuma did not fight the invaders, but simply gave his throne to Cortés.

Stone skull rack

This stone carving *(right)* shows a rack of human skulls. Each pyramid temple had a real skull rack for holding the heads of sacrificed prisoners. The Spanish invaders were horrified to find a rack at Tenochtitlan that held some ten thousand skulls. They thought the Aztecs were totally barbaric.

Stone statues at El Templo Mayor
Each of these stone statues *(above)* has a hole in its chest in the heart area, showing that the Aztecs removed the hearts of the humans they sacrificed.

Modern Mexico City
Mexico City is the capital of Mexico. Tenochtitlan's ruins lie buried under the modern city. The cathedral near the center of this picture *(above)* was built partly with Aztec stones. It was completed in the 1800s.

MODERN PYRAMIDS

HAVE you ever seen a modern pyramid-shaped building? Most of them look like pyramids on the outside but, inside, they are just like other buildings. Ancient pyramids were built from earth or stones piled up to make huge mounds. Modern pyramids are much smaller and lighter. Instead of huge stone blocks, they are made from concrete, steel, and glass. Inside, modern pyramids have steel frames, like strong skeletons, to support concrete slabs that form the outside walls. There is something about a pyramid shape that still impresses people and gets their attention. People today, just like the people of ancient Egypt or Central America, will often choose a pyramid when they want something special.

Forge shopping center, Glasgow
This pyramid-shaped shopping center *(above)* is in Glasgow, Scotland. Today, all over the world, quite a few buildings, such as offices, banks, and hotels, are pyramid-shaped.

The Louvre, Paris, France
This glass pyramid *(left)*, built around the entrance to the famous Louvre museum, was completed in 1989. Its sides slope at the same angle as the Great Pyramid at Giza. This picture shows an interesting view of the pyramid reflected in water at night. Many people admire this bold new building, even though it is so different from the older museum next to it.

Luxor Hotel, Las Vegas

This pyramid *(right),* built in 1993 by an American businessman, houses a hotel and gambling casino, complete with waiters dressed as Egyptian pharaohs. Its main framework is steel girders covered with black glass. In front of the hotel is a copy of the famous Sphinx, made of plastic and concrete.

Transamerica building, San Francisco

The Transamerica pyramid skyscraper *(left)* is 840 feet (256 m) high. San Francisco is an area where there is a danger of earthquakes. Because a pyramid is a stable shape, the Transamerica building's pyramid-shaped steel frame helps it withstand tremors.

Sadat Memorial, Cairo, Egypt

The Egyptian president Muhammad Anwar al Sadat was killed in 1981 near this pyramid-shaped memorial to Egyptian soldiers. Sadat is buried here.

FACT BOX

• A glass building that is shaped like a pyramid traps warmth from the sun, just like a greenhouse. The solar heat keeps the building warm naturally.

• Glass pyramids must be fitted with outside rails on which mountaineering window cleaners can clip their safety harnesses.

USING PYRAMID SHAPES

WHEN you are standing up in a bus or train that is shaking as it moves along, how do you keep yourself from falling over? You probably spread your feet apart so you are wider at the bottom than at the top — just like a pyramid. The pyramid shape is very stable and rigid, so it does not easily bend or buckle. High-tension towers are extremely good examples of a modern use of pyramid shapes. They have a square base and sloping sides, which support the heavy cables that carry electricity to our homes, offices, and factories. The pyramid shape of high-tension towers makes them able to withstand even hurricane-force winds. Pyramid shapes also help hold up buildings. The Transamerica pyramid building in San Francisco is like a huge high-tension tower covered with concrete. From towers to skyscrapers to egg cartons, the pyramid is an important shape that has many valuable uses in modern life.

The symbol for the British television station Anglia TV (above) is pyramid-shaped. This shape is very effective because people recognize and remember it easily.

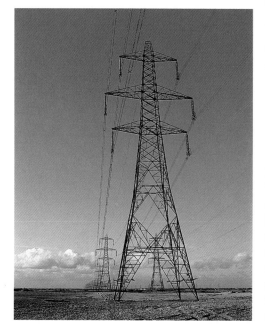

High-tension tower
The tapering pyramid shape of a high-tension tower makes it very stable. It is designed to use the least amount of metal to create the greatest possible strength. The electricity cables are attached to long glass insulators that hang down from the steel arms of the tower.

FACT BOX

• A large egg carton made of papier mâché will probably support your weight if you step on it — very carefully — because the pyramid shape is so strong, rigid, and stable.

• Large high-tension towers are about 100 feet (30 m) tall, but their pyramid shape keeps them strong and stable even in high winds.

• One of the first trademarks ever used was a red, triangular pyramid shape. It was used by a brewery.

Egg-carton shapes

Egg cartons *(right)* have paper or plastic pyramid shapes arranged side by side. They can hold a chicken's egg of any size. Each egg slips downward until it is held by the sloping sides of the four pyramids surrounding each hole. Trays of eggs can be stacked, one on top of the other, without breaking a single egg.

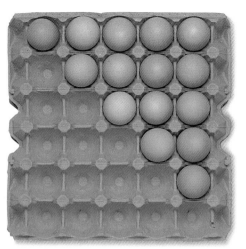

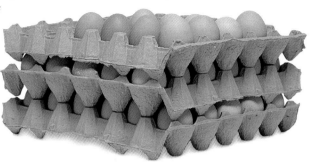

Obelisk shapes

This movie set *(below)* was built for a film about Cleopatra, a famous queen of ancient Egypt. In it, you can see another kind of ancient pyramid shape — the obelisk — a tall column with a small pyramid at the top. Obelisks were originally used as monuments or for religious purposes.

World War II tank traps

These concrete, flat-topped pyramids *(above)* were placed in open ground during World War II. The idea was that the tracks of enemy tanks would slip down the sides, trapping the tanks.

BUILDING WITH PYRAMIDS

*You will need:
cardboard or thick paper,
scissors, pencil, white glue,
ruler, weight (such as
a small package).*

THE pyramid is a strong, versatile shape, so there are many uses for it, some of which have already been illustrated. Just as in ancient times, pyramids are still used in building, especially in areas of the world where there is a danger of earthquakes. Earthquakes make the ground shake violently and can cause buildings to topple over. The people who design buildings, or architects, have found that pyramid-shaped frames inside buildings can help keep them from collapsing. The project on this page shows more proof of how strong and stable pyramid shapes can be. It also shows how you can fit pyramid shapes together to form other shapes — and then discover what properties these new shapes have. The project on the opposite page compares pyramids with box shapes of exactly the same height and base size. See for yourself which shape is better at resisting violent shaking.

Learning about shapes

1 Make twelve identical cardboard pyramids. The sloping faces must be at 45° angles, which means that the pyramid's height should equal half the diagonal measurement across its base.

2 Make one big pyramid from six small ones *(as shown)*. There will be gaps around the edges. Then, make one big cube from six small pyramids, gluing the pyramids together.

3 Try balancing weight on both the pyramid and the cube. They are equally strong. The pyramid shape is strong even though it has gaps in it. The cube, unlike the cube on page 9, is strong because it is made up of pyramid shapes.

Make a mini-earthquake

1 With a type of modeling clay that is not too sticky, make a small cube and a pyramid. They must both be the same height and their bases must be the same size.

2 Place the cube and the pyramid on a book. Slowly tilt the book to imitate the effect of an earthquake. The cube topples over long before the pyramid does.

3 The shapes you have just tested were low to the ground. Try making and testing two taller shapes. As before, they must both have the same height and base size.

MATERIALS
You will need:
modeling clay, spatula, book.

4 Do the book test again. You should find that the pyramid is the more stable shape. It is the second of the two shapes to fall over.

Kobe, Japan
These houses collapsed during an earthquake in Kobe, Japan. Buildings with pyramid-shaped frames are less likely to suffer this kind of damage.

PYRAMIDS AND CHEMISTRY

SOME of the pyramids you have seen so far, such as the Great Pyramid at Giza, in Egypt, are among the largest manufactured objects in the world. There are, however, other pyramids that are much, much smaller and are found where you might not expect to find pyramids at all. Some of these pyramids are so tiny you need a magnifying glass or a microscope to see them. They are called crystals. You can find them in some everyday substances. For example, look closely at a spoonful of sugar or salt, and you will see thousands of tiny crystals, each one shaped like a cube. Other crystals are shaped like tetrahedrons or square pyramids. Crystals are often found deep underground, inside minerals, or rocks. These minerals formed millions of years ago, when molten rock cooled slowly and changed from a liquid into a solid. As the rocks cooled, the crystals grew larger. Crystals are not just beautiful to look at; they also have many practical uses.

The shape of this crystal of calcite (above) is like two square pyramids joined together at the base, so it is called a bipyramid.

Quartz

This picture *(right)* shows crystals of the mineral quartz. Tiny slivers of these pyramid-shaped crystals are used in quartz clocks and watches. The quartz controls the speed at which an electric current switches on and off, which, in turn, controls how fast the hands turn around.

FACT BOX

• There are six basic types, or shapes, of crystals, called crystal systems.

• All the crystals of a particular substance normally have the same shape.

• Diamonds and graphite (used in most lead pencils) are both forms of pure carbon, but they have different crystal structures.

• Diamonds formed millions of years ago, when carbon was heated and squeezed deep underneath volcanoes.

Sulfur

Sulfur crystals *(right)* grow inside the craters of volcanoes. There are two types of sulfur crystals: dipyramid-shaped orthorhombic sulfur and column-shaped monoclinic sulfur. Millions of tons of sulfur are used each year to make sulfuric acid, used in paint, plant fertilizers, detergents, and some plastics.

Volcanoes and crystals

The smoke rising from this volcano *(below)* contains sulfur gas that comes from deep underground. As the gas touches a sulfur crystal, it cools, solidifies, and builds up an extra layer on the surface of the crystal.

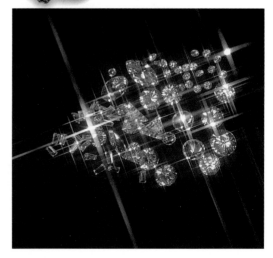

Diamonds

These diamonds have been cut and polished to form beautiful gemstones. The carbon inside diamonds is arranged in tetrahedral patterns.

GROW PYRAMID CRYSTALS

*You will need:
small shallow tray (make a
simple one from cardboard or
use the lid of a shoebox),
marbles of 5 different colors.*

EVERYTHING around us is made up of tiny particles called atoms. Different things are made up of different atoms, arranged in different ways. Any particular crystal consists of atoms arranged in a regular, repeating pattern. This regular pattern inside a crystal gives it its consistent outer shape, which is why, no matter what their size, most crystals of a particular substance have exactly the same shape. Crystals form from gases, liquids, or solutions that are cooling slowly. They increase in size when more and more atoms from the cooling gas or liquid add themselves to the surface of the crystal. In the project on this page, you can make a model of a crystal and see how the atoms build up inside it. Note that the model crystal you will make is a square pyramid because you will be using a tray with four sides. Also, keep in mind that crystals grow in all directions, not just upward. The project on the opposite page shows a simple way to grow real crystals from a liquid solution.

Make a crystal model

3 Add two more layers of marbles to make a complete crystal model.

1 Layer marbles in the tray in a square pattern. Each atom is touching eight others. In some substances, atoms are arranged in a hexagon (six-sided) pattern, each one touching six others.

2 Add a second and a third layer. Each marble sits in a dip between four marbles in the layer below. Each marble in the third layer is directly above a marble in the very first layer.

Grow your own crystals

1 Ask an adult to pour 1 cup (240 ml) of very hot water into a pitcher. Add a spoonful of dishwashing soap powder and stir until it all dissolves. Add more soap until no more dissolves.

2 Dissolving a solid in a liquid makes a solution. When no more solid will dissolve, the solution is said to be saturated. Pour the solution into a bowl. (Leave undissolved solids in the pitcher.)

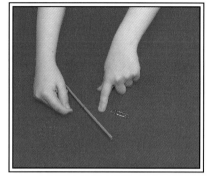

3 A crystal needs a place to grow. Attach a paper clip to a drinking straw with a piece of thread. Make the distance from the straw to the paper clip about two-thirds the depth of the bowl.

MATERIALS

You will need: hot water, pitcher, spoon, dishwashing soap powder, bowl, paper clip, drinking straw, thread, magnifying glass.

WARNING
Do not rub your eyes when touching chemicals. Wash your hands after each step.

4 As some of the water evaporates, there will not be enough to keep all the solids dissolved. Some will appear on the paper clip, and a clump of crystals will start to grow.

5 After several days, there will be a large clump of crystals growing on the paper clip. Remove the paper clip and crystals from the solution and wash them quickly under cold water. Look closely at the crystals through a magnifying glass. You should be able to see that the shapes of the crystals are all the same.

STAIRWAYS TO HEAVEN

THE pyramids of ancient Egypt reached into the sky as stairways for the souls of their dead kings. The pyramid is the perfect shape to focus our gaze on the sky above. Throughout history, however, other peoples have built differently shaped buildings for the same purpose. At the same time the ancient Egyptians were building pyramids, the Sumerians, Babylonians, and other Mesopotamians were building towers called ziggurats. These peoples lived in the land that is now Iraq, about 600 miles (965 km) northeast of Egypt. Ziggurats were like stepped pyramids. They reached up into the sky so that priests could be closer to their gods. All over the world, throughout history, different peoples have reached toward the skies because they believe that their gods live in heaven and that their souls go to heaven when their bodies die.

A caller, or muezzin, summons people to prayer from the top of a minaret.

Great ziggurat, Ur, now Iraq
This platform *(below)* is the lowest part of the ziggurat at Ur. It has been restored. Most ancient ziggurats were built of brick and crumbled long ago.

Minaret, Samarra, Iraq
This spiral minaret *(left)* is 170 feet (52 m) high. A minaret is a type of tower. You will find minarets in countries where Islam is the main religion. A person known as a muezzin calls out from the top of a minaret several times a day to tell the faithful that it is time to pray.

The Tower of Babel

This picture *(left)* was painted in 1563 by Pieter Brueghel. According to the Bible, people tried to build this ziggurat near Babylon to reach heaven. God stopped them by making each person speak a different language, so they could not understand each other. This story became one explanation of how so many different languages came into the world.

Steep-sided, sloping shape

Pyramid at Meroe, Sudan, Africa

This pyramid *(right)* was built by Nubian kings about 2,000 years ago. Like the Egyptians, the Nubians built pyramid tombs to make sure their souls would have a path to heaven.

Brihadeshwara temple, India

These temples *(above)* are at Thanjavur, in southern India. Each pyramid-shaped roof is covered with intricate carvings of characters and ideas from Hindu legends.

MYTHS AND MYSTERIES

PYRAMIDS date from the earliest times of human civilization. Much about them is mysterious, and many of the questions cannot be answered. Over the centuries, right up to the present, amazing stories have appeared that try to explain these mysteries. For example, how did the ancient Egyptians, the Maya, and the Aztecs move such enormous stones to build their pyramids? Some people say that visitors from outer space helped move the stones. Look at the sarcophagus lid from the tomb at Palenque (page 41). One person suggested that it shows a spaceman taking off in a rocket. There are hundreds of other stories of this kind.

However far-fetched the myths about pyramids, this simple shape has become a powerful symbol to everybody. It represents age, wisdom, and something solid and truly long lasting. More than anything else, however, the shape represents mystery — and we probably will never understand it completely.

Pyramid tomb, 1798–1806
This pyramid was attached to the tomb of Austrian Archduchess Marie Christine. In the late 1700s and early 1800s, pyramid-shaped tombs were fashionable in Europe. Perhaps this was partly because the Egyptian pyramid stands for the idea of life continuing after death.

In 1970, Thor Heyerdahl sailed this copy of an ancient Egyptian boat (above) from Africa to Central America. Some people think this journey proves that Egyptians crossed the Atlantic and taught the Maya to build pyramids. The pyramids in the Americas, however, didn't appear until much later than those in Egypt. Also, people in different regions can often come up with the same ideas.

PYRAMID MYTHS

• A blunt knife becomes sharp if it is put under a pyramid!

• Pyramid-shaped hats improve a person's thinking power.

• Imhotep, who designed Djoser's step pyramid at Sakkara, Egypt, came from Antarctica!

Joseph's Granaries

This mosaic *(right)* is in St. Mark's Chapel in Venice, Italy. The scene is from a tale of the Bible in which Joseph predicts a famine in Egypt and advises the king to store food. Because of this story, some people in the Middle Ages thought the Egyptian pyramids were actually granaries, which are buildings used to store grain and other foods.

Charles Piazzi Smyth

Charles Piazzi Smyth

During the 1800s, a Scotsman named Charles Piazzi Smyth produced detailed measurements of Khufu's pyramid at Giza *(left)*. Smyth claimed that the measurements were like a calendar. Based on his theories, he also made predictions about miracles that would take place in the future. None of his predictions has come true.

GLOSSARY

Anubis – the Egyptian god of embalming who had the head of a jackal on a human body.

archaeologist – a scientist who digs up and examines the material remains of the lives and activities of people in past cultures and ancient times.

barbaric – not civilized; wild, almost savage.

binder – a substance, such as glue or tar, used to hold loose materials together.

bitumen – a natural, carbon substance sometimes used as a binder. The word "mummy" was derived from the Arabic name for this substance.

calcite – the mineral calcium carbonate, commonly found as limestone, marble, or chalk.

canopic jar – a covered stone or pottery container in which the soft internal organs of the deceased in ancient Egypt were preserved for burial.

carbon – a nonmetallic chemical element found in all plants and animals and in many nonliving substances, such as asphalt, oil, and charcoal.

causeway – a raised road or highway that crosses low or uneven ground.

cenote – a deep hole or cavern in limestone with a pool of water at the bottom.

crystal – a chemical element or combination of elements hardened into a solid with a particular number and arrangement of flat surfaces.

embalming – treating a dead body with chemicals to keep it from decaying.

encased – closed in on all sides as if in a case.

fulcrum – the supporting structure, or prop, on which a lever pivots, or turns, when lifting a load.

geometry – a kind of mathematics that deals with shapes, lines, and angles.

habits – the particular shapes of different crystals.

hieroglyph – a character in the ancient Egyptian system of writing with pictures.

igneous – formed beneath Earth's surface, or in volcanoes, by fire or intense heat.

jackal – a wolflike wild dog found mostly in Asian and African regions.

metamorphic – changed in structure by natural forces, such as pressure or heat, to become harder and more crystallike.

minaret – a tall, thin tower next to a Muslim mosque, or place of worship, from which a muezzin calls people to prayer.

mortuary – a place where the deceased are prepared for burial; a funeral home.

muezzin – a Muslim who calls people to prayer.

mummy – a dead body preserved by embalming and other burial procedures used by the ancient Egyptians.

natron – a natural salt used in the ancient process of embalming.

obelisk – a four-sided pillar with a pyramid-shaped top.

pharaoh – the title of a ruler or king in ancient Egypt.

pigment – a powdery substance that creates color when mixed with a liquid.

plumb – (n) a line or cord with a weight attached, used to test the straightness of a structure's vertical, or up and down, direction.

preservation – the act of keeping something in good condition, protecting it from damage or decay.

quarry – a place where rock and stone are found in large masses and are removed from the earth by digging, cutting, and blasting.

quartz – a common mineral containing silicon dioxide that occurs in either masses or hexagonal crystals that can be colored or colorless.

Re – the Egyptian god of the Sun who had the head of a falcon on a human body.

resin – a sticky, or sappy, substance that comes from trees and other plants and does not dissolve in water.

ritual – an organized series of activities; a ceremony.

rubble – rough fragments of stones or bricks and broken pieces of other solid materials.

sarcophagus – a large stone coffin, often decorated with carvings, used by the ancient Egyptians to bury kings.

seal – a closure that readily reveals tampering because it has to be broken to be opened.

sedimentary – formed by deposits of materials moved by wind, water, and glaciers.

sledge – a big, heavy vehicle that moves along on runners, like a sled, and is used to carry large loads of materials or many people.

spinel – a crystallike mineral that is found in a range of colors and is used like a gemstone.

sulfur – a nonmetallic chemical element found in Earth's crust, especially in volcanic regions, that is easily recognized by its "rotten egg" smell.

tessellation – the act of fitting together geometric shapes so they cover a defined area without any gaps between them or any overlapping.

tetrahedron – a triangular pyramid with four faces: a base and three sides.

ziggurat – a pyramidlike tower, found in Mesopotamian countries, that was built in stages, like steps, with a temple or shrine on top.

BOOKS

Building Technology. Technology in Action (series).
Mark Lambert (Franklin Watts)

An Egyptian Pyramid. Inside Story (series).
Jacqueline Morley (Peter Bedrick Books)

Great Pyramid: The Story of the Farmers, the God-King, and the Most Astounding Structure Ever Built.
Elizabeth B. Mann (Mikaya Press)

Make This Egyptian Mummy. Cut-out Models (series).
Iain Ashman (EDC)

The Master Builders. Mysterious Places (series).
Philip Wilkinson (Chelsea House)

Mummies. Weird & Wacky Science (series).
Ron Knapp (Enslow Publishers)

Pyramid. James Putnam (Alfred A. Knopf)

The Pyramids: The Latest Secrets Revealed in the Light of Recent Scientific Discoveries. Anne Millard
(Millbrook Press)

Pyramids: Opposing Viewpoints. Michael O'Neal
(GreenHaven Press)

Pyramids and Temples. Superstructures (series).
Jane Parker (Raintree Steck-Vaughn)

Structures. Bernie Zubrowski
(Cuisenaire Company of America)

Structures and Buildings. New Technology (series).
Nigel Hawkes (TFC Books)

VIDEOS

The Great Pyramid. (A&E Home Video)

The Maya: Temples, Tombs, and Time.
(Knowledge Unlimited, Inc.)

Mysteries of the Pyramids. (Karol Video)

Pyramids. (PBS Home Video)

Pyramids of Mexico: Sentinels of Silence
(Educational Video Network)

Shape Hunting: Cylinders, Prisms, and Pyramids.
(Coronet/MTI Film & Video)

This Old Pyramid. (Knowledge Unlimited, Inc.)

WEB SITES

www.pbs.org/wgbh/nova/pyramid   www2.torstar.com/rom/egypt

Some web sites stay current longer than others. For further web sites, use your search engines to locate the following topics: *burial, Chichén Itzá, Egypt, Giza, hieroglyphs, mummy, pharaoh, temples, Teotihuacan, tombs.*

INDEX

PICTURE CREDITS